*Portrait of the Artist
as a Brown Man*

# Portrait of the Artist as a Brown Man

≡ *poems* ≡

## Jose Hernandez Diaz

Benjamin Saltman
Poetry Award
Winner

Red Hen Press | *Pasadena, CA*

Book design by Mark E. Cull

Library of Congress Cataloging-in-Publication Data

Names: Hernandez Diaz, Jose (Poet), author.
Title: Portrait of the artist as a brown man: poems / Jose Hernandez Diaz.
Other titles: Portrait of the artist as a brown man (Compilation)
Description: First edition. | Pasadena, CA: Red Hen Press, 2025.
Identifiers: LCCN 2024018728 (print) | LCCN 2024018729 (ebook) | ISBN 9781636282404 (trade paperback) | ISBN 9781636282497 (hardback) | ISBN 9781636282411 (ebook)
Subjects: LCGFT: Poetry.
Classification: LCC PS3608.E7685 P67 2025 (print) | LCC PS3608.E7685 (ebook) | DDC 811/.6—dc23/eng/20240722
LC record available at https://lccn.loc.gov/2024018728
LC ebook record available at https://lccn.loc.gov/2024018729

Publication of this book has been made possible in part through the generous financial support of Ann Beman.

The National Endowment for the Arts, the Los Angeles County Arts Commission, the Ahmanson Foundation, the Dwight Stuart Youth Fund, the Max Factor Family Foundation, the Pasadena Tournament of Roses Foundation, the Pasadena Arts & Culture Commission and the City of Pasadena Cultural Affairs Division, the City of Los Angeles Department of Cultural Affairs, the Audrey & Sydney Irmas Charitable Foundation, the Meta & George Rosenberg Foundation, the Albert and Elaine Borchard Foundation, the Adams Family Foundation, Amazon Literary Partnership, the Sam Francis Foundation, and the Mara W. Breech Foundation partially support Red Hen Press.

   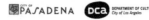 

First Edition
Published by Red Hen Press
www.redhen.org

## ACKNOWLEDGEMENTS

Grateful acknowledgement is made to the following literary journals where some of these poems first appeared, sometimes in different forms:

*Assignment Magazine, Astrolabe, Bennington Review, Border Crossing* (CAN), *Brazos River Review, Broken Lens Journal, Cincinnati Review, Copihue Poetry, Diode Poetry Journal, Double Yolk, Empty Mirror, Ghost City Review, Guesthouse Lit, The Hooghly Review* (India), *Hoot Review, Hoxie Gorge Review, Inscape Journal, The International Literary Quarterly, Leavings Lit Mag, Leon Literary Review, Los Angeles Review, The Missouri Review, Moot Point Magazine, Moria Literary Magazine, North American Review, Northwest Review, On The Seawall, Poem-A-Day Series, Poetry Wales* (UK), *Quarter After Eight, Rogue Agent, The Rumpus, Salamander Magazine, Small Orange, South Dakota Review, The Southern Review, South Florida Poetry Journal, Tahoma Literary Review, TriQuarterly, Whale Road Review.*

# Contents

⇒ I ⇐

## ⇒ II ⇐

## ⇒ III ⇐

## ⟶ IV ⟜

*Portrait of the Artist
as a Brown Man*

≡ I ≡

## Portrait of the Artist as a Brown Man

A few years ago, I was in the same library,
In the same quiet, upper-middle-class town

I didn't live in. I'd just finished writing
A prose poem that would eventually

Get published in *The Nation*. Writer's high.
Then, a white lady came up to me

And asked about the trash. I was confused,
Until I realized she thought

I was a janitor.

*Hey,*

With the intention of abandoning the hierarchies of capitalism—
The machinery of thought. Hey, with the desire of growing lilacs
In our community garden, bougainvillea running along the wall.
Hey, as we denounce the walls of isolation and marginalization.
No, to the elite. No, to centuries of settler colonialism,
Their insistence, we are immigrants on our own land.
Hey, at midnight, beneath the candle of the moon: our arms
Interlocked like laurels painted onto the rims of renaissance paintings.
Hey, I miss you. I never even met you: let's take a deep dive
Into each other's bookshelves, until we find oceans of imagery
And metaphors we can discuss, dissect, not for ego's sake, but for love.

## Ode to Brown Skin

People assume I want to be lighter. Never crossed my mind. I know I'm indigenous and strong. Like my ancestors, proud and wise. Do not assume I will rob or murder you when I walk behind you, in a parking lot, late at night. Do not assume I'm a high school dropout, or in gangs. Even though the Spanish channel prefers light-skinned actors, I'm not fooled by the shaky lens. Typically, Mexican families have instructed their children to marry lighter skinned folks. But I can see above the noise. Above the hate. The hate we can't live without. The hate we love. Brown skin, like pan dulce. Brown skin, like la tierra. Brown skin, like a tortilla. Brown skin, ancient armor.

## *Ode to the Pollo Asado Burritos from Alberto's Tacos*

I am faithful to you. Faithful, like the sun and moon. I howl like
a Mexican Ranchera singer when I'm hangry for you. Just enough
guacamole, pico de gallo, pollo asado to satisfy my existential
crisis about the Lakers, but never over-the-top spicy. Not trying to
prove a point. Just right, like the weather in Southern California.
Just right, like the temperature of the ocean at dawn in the
summertime, before a surf session. I used to prefer the Carne
Asada or California Burrito, but I'm getting older now and must
consider things like health, weight, and not dying of a heart
attack. Mis saludos to the Mexican chef at Alberto's who always
balances the burrito with just the right amount of duende into
the homemade tortillas de harina. Also, let me get a can of Coca-
Cola with that, not diet, for once, regular. I'll live a little, today,
with a classic can of cola, reminiscent of childhood summertime
visits to Mexico to see the familia. Only once per week, though,
like attending to the rising pile of laundry, like Rams games, like
going to the library on Sunday afternoon, in La Habra, to the
only library that's open, to read a cozy book or write a jazzy prose
poem. Perhaps a prose poem about the Pollo Asado burritos from
Alberto's Tacos, where they never disappoint and never-ever close,
not even holidays.

*Ode to Pan Dulce con Café*

I don't get to eat you as much as I want for health reasons.
But when I do, I savor each bite like a religious ritual.
Subtly sweet; tender. The nostalgia of youth

when mom would come home from Gonzalez Market
with many grocery bags. "Traje pan dulce," she'd say.
I'd rush to the table, coffee on the stove,

pick up the puerquito and a pink concha.
The pan is like fine artisan work. Reminders of youth,
but also, of the motherland: México, where I've

only been on vacation, but always felt like a second home.

## Ode to Agua de Jamaica

An essential cold drink at a mom-and-pop Mexican restaurant.
Best served in the summertime heat waves of Mid-August.

Plenty of solid ice cubes to dilute the sharp bitterness.
Best consumed with tacos de asada or burritos de pollo asado.

Are you from Jamaica or Latin America, saccharine thirst-quencher?
I found you in my barrio at a local Mexican restaurant,

Southeast of Los Angeles, west of Americana.
I remember drinking you from a plastic bag with a straw,

While visiting my Abuelitos in Guanajuato, México,
During summertime visits while on break from school.

Such a rich, refreshing, vibrant red beverage.

## *Ode to the Piñata*

You're always there for me, dear piñata. Every year you greet me
when I need you most. When I'm one year closer to death. You
remind me to take a second and enjoy dulces. You have a deep
philosophy: swing; swing harder; eat candy. What utter wisdom.
Sartre himself would be proud. Piñata, your colors are as majestic
as a rainbow, swaying in the sky. Sure, I'm fully grown and don't
need you anymore. But you bring me happiness and dammit
that's important. No, I don't eat candy anymore, but a chocolate
or two won't hurt. Besides, seeing my sobrinos run to get
scattered dulces is worth any price or trouble. Maybe I will put a
bouquet of carnations inside of you, sweet piñata? Maybe a dozen
tacos de asada? Al pastor? All kidding aside, you've been in our
familia since the beginning, even before Los Abuelitos. I know
you'll stick around till the end. The end, when the merry world
explodes, like a spinning piñata.

## *Ode to the Melting of I.C.E.*

Just leave already. You're too old in your ways.
No one likes you. How do you look yourself in the mirror?

Why do you treat people like that? Have you no conscience?
It is foolish to even suggest you might have one.

You do not own the land. You can never own the land.
Why don't you melt away in the summer sun?

Why don't you melt away in the summer sun?
You incite hate in the eyes of your citizens.

You justify murder and rape and cages.
Go away and never come back.

Go away, it's better like that.

## Ode to My Emiliano Zapata Tattoo

I got you in my early twenties. It felt macho
yet romantic. Perhaps it could scare white people away.

General Zapata was a martyr, yes, but he was no victim.
A man who arose to take arms against his oppressors.

Now, in my late 30's, I look at you, Zapata tattoo,
and wonder what is next? Perhaps a skeleton? A rose?

A Mariachi? Perhaps a skeleton Mariachi, with a rose?
I chose to paint my body with Mexican and Chicano imagery

to remember my roots, to venerate my culture,
because the body is the ultimate canvas,

tattoos like little poems in a priceless book.

## Ode to Boxing

You're always there for me on the weekend
when I need a good show. Something to root for,

with a beer in hand and the company of cousins,
shouting, cheering at the spectacle. I want to see

a Mexican fighter showing bravery, skill,
and a victory. I want to see myself reflected in Brown men

with Aztec tattoos and short fade haircuts, like mine.
Sure, it can get violent. The world is also violent. But,

there is plenty of technique which takes years to master.
Moving and sticking. These working-class men

come from backgrounds like mine. Tough barrios like mine,
with Spanish last names like mine. For now, Monday morning,

the work week just beginning, watch my fancy footwork and jab,
as I swing like a hungry underdog aiming for a title.

*Ode to Mrs. Weir*

Thank you to my high school English teacher, Mrs. Weir,
For introducing me to literature. I remember reading

*The Catcher in the Rye* during junior year of high school,
And hearing Holden speak in an everyday manner,

And it spoke to me, along with his rebellious spirit,
Angsty teenager that I was. But it wasn't just Salinger's

Genius that led me to literature. It was the way Mrs. Weir
Talked about writing and art; writing was something of dignity,

And sophistication. I saw videos of Camus in black-and-white
In a beret and thought, that could be me. I could write like that.

I could stand like that. I could look away from the camera, just like that.
I remember the last day of school, senior year, going to Mrs. Weir's

Class for one last time, for her to sign my yearbook. She wrote that
I could be anything I wanted: a lawyer, writer, a teacher. Anything.

I remember crying that night, because I didn't know if I would ever see her
Again. Thank you, Mrs. Weir, for changing my life. Thank you for teaching

Me to love literature, and, more importantly, life.

*Ode to My Parents Who Immigrated from México*

Sometimes, I feel guilty for having been born first-generation
Mexican-American. My parents went through a lot

for my siblings and I. Crossing a massive, deadly border,
entering a country without knowing the language, culture,

working tedious jobs for endless hours. Guilty, for having it easier,
though not compared to my American friends, growing up.

They didn't really know about hand-me-downs, free lunches,
getting hit with a belt for saying curse words in both English

and Spanish. Still, my parents and other immigrants sacrificed
leaving their families behind, being despised by Americans,

for simply seeking a better life of hope. Yet, they never complain.
They're not perfect, no, but if you want to see the true strength

of America, it's in the rough hands, bright eyes,
and in the frank smiles of immigrants.

## El Café Duende

The café is spinning jazz—
Cigarette smoke rises and crashes
with the abstract pattern in my mind:
Lilac wind. Autumn moon.
There is a dusty window in the bohemian room,
and you walk through it. The blue rain
softly falls in the dark street,
and you walk through it.

## Lunar Café

I like just sitting here in this cozy café
with you beneath the moon. Cigarettes lit,
     coffee cups spilled to fill with European vodka.

Look at the subtle way in which the abstract painting
on the wall glistens. You are prettier still.
     In a more direct and profound way.

I like just sitting here in this cozy café,
with you, beneath the moon. Your eyes
     are like kissable stars and your lips

     they seem almost unreachable.

*The Last Time I Saw You*

I'm reading Rosario Castellanos
     in the library almond eyes

          remind me of yours summer moon

     ardent night lush lips appear on the page
          it's been three weeks since you

          left the café at 2 a.m. the plane

never landed in Mexico City
     it circulates my thoughts it circulates

          my thoughts looking for a place to land

I offer my open palms
     won't keep still love kiss soul

## The Last Time I Cried

Was when I was watching Misty Copeland
dance The Nutcracker on mute,
As I listened to "The Point of No Return"
by Immortal Technique.

It was simply beautiful.
What other words could I use?
Fierce. Elegant. Magical.
The thought that she grew up
near my neighborhood,

And grew up low-income, like me,
makes me feel a kinship to her.
I always knew ballet was an art,
and appreciated the movements,

But the music always threw me off
as a little boring. The last time I cried,
While watching Misty dance
to Immortal Technique, it felt so good

To cry to something beautiful for once.
Like I wasn't alone, anymore.
Like ballet and poetry and hip-hop,
it's all the same, same window to love.

Watching Misty dance to the
underground hip-hop of my youth,
I feel as though I've united two worlds;
two tiny, brilliant worlds.

*Why Does Kafkaesque Nonsense Always Happen to Me?*

I'm getting billed for a Fall 2022 semester at Denver Community College. The problem is I've never enrolled, nor have I ever been to Denver, Colorado. Why does Kafkaesque nonsense always happen to me? Sometimes, I feel like just throwing in the towel. The pugilist life isn't for me. I'm a lover not a cage fighter. I should've been a famous ballerino or playwright. There's enough drama in my life to write a new literary canon. The gloomy existential novel I'm currently living is called, "Why Does Kafkaesque Nonsense Always Happen to Me?'

*20 alternative careers to academic poet*

1. Big wave surfer.

2. Avant-garde saxophonist.

3. Pastry chef.

4. Memoirist.

5. Governor of Absurdism.

6. Retired clergy.

7. Shortstop for the Dodgers.

8. Professor of Paletas Michoacánas.

9. Librarian, Librarian, Librarian.

10. Scarecrow.

11. Lead guitarist for The Mars Volta.

12. Government spy.

13. Statue in the park.

14. Prima Ballerina.

15. Jean-Paul Sartre's ghost.

16. Bodyguard for Pablo Neruda.

17. An idea with humorous appeal.

18. Doctor of Generosity.

19. Un cotorro en la selva.

20. Una memoria de lluvia.

*Who's that you're looking for?*

Does her name begin with x?
　　　　I don't know if it'll rain.
　　　　　　　The weatherman says 60% chance.
　　　　This is the last time we'll speak.
As lovers. We may remain friends.
　　　　What's your favorite continent?
　　　　　　　Mine's North America. Stop shouting.
　　　　We're inches away. Inches. Away,
we fell like something other than sunset.
　　　　Unbeautiful. The next bus arrives at 11:15.
　　　　　　　It's also the last bus. Hurry up. Wait.
　　　　Timing isn't everything. Power is everything.
Power and politics. Whatever.
　　　　Don't pretend to miss me,
　　　　　　　all you really need is Netflix and
　　　a couple scoops of pistachio ice cream.

## Portrait of a Jogger with a Toucan in Southeast Los Angeles

I was in the middle of my Sunday morning jog at the local park
when suddenly a majestic, colorful toucan made an appearance
by the rusty water fountain. I was shocked. Was I suddenly in
South America? Better yet, was I suddenly in a South American
rainforest? Of course not. I was in the southeast suburbs of Los
Angeles. I began to wonder if a toucan had escaped from the
local zoo or maybe someone had stashed it as an illegal pet and
it got away? Regardless, I needed my phone to take a photo. As I
fumbled through my pockets for the phone, the toucan somehow
disappeared, perhaps flying back home. Disappointed I didn't get
the photo I wanted, I decided to stop everything, rush to Michael's
for a canvas, and paint the toucan in a Los Angeles park in order
to preserve its pure memory. I painted the ancient toucan with
a bright blue and neon-yellow beak, perched onto a seedy water
fountain, next to a graffiti-laced handball court. I then painted
the bright sun and a palatero with a sombrero in the background
beneath lush palm trees. Lastly, I drew myself jogging at the
park in my Dodgers hat, next to the toucan. I titled the painting,
"Portrait of a Jogger with a Toucan in Southeast Los Angeles."

## Abuelita

*Para mi abuelita, Amalia Guzman*

My abuelita is visiting from México.
　　When the sun goes down and it starts

To get dark out, she always says,
　　"Esta oscuro como la boca de un lobo."

Dark like a wolf's mouth. She is getting
　　Older now, eighty-nine years old. She can't

Really cook for herself anymore. I try to
　　Help as much as I can. She's the best.

Yesterday, my brother asked her where
　　She was born: *Guanajuato or Michoacán?*

She said Michoacán. She said the last time
　　She went to the rancho where she was born

Was a couple of years ago, but she didn't have
　　A good time because it rained and rained.

I think, maybe they are tears from the sky.
　　Tears or rain of celebration for her return.

But, I wouldn't say such a sentimental thing to her face,
    Because she's been hardened by life as an orphan,

Then getting married and my abuelo dies in his forties;
    Having to raise eleven kids on her own. No, I don't say anything,

But I picture her at her childhood home, sitting on the porch,
    Watching the rainfall, wishing her comadres would come by,

Most of them dead now, then one of them would say,
    *Hola, ¿Como estas, Doña Amalia? Tantos años han pasado.*

*Almost Buried*

When my twin brother tells me stories about hanging out
With his cholo gangster friends from high school, part of me

Doesn't want to hear it. It's not that I'm afraid: I'm afraid to admit
That I'm afraid and I play along. He doesn't tell me to show off,

That's for sure. He's not necessarily trying to scare me.
I think he's just remembering his time with his friends;

The few that he had. They all came from broken homes.
Their parents were drug addicts. Lived in low-rent apartments,

Like us. None of his friends ever brought their drama
To our home. Didn't say bad words in front of my parents.

They were boys hiding behind baggy shirts and pants,
Because the world didn't think much of them to ever

Give them a chance. I guess the reason I don't like to hear
His stories, even though it's good for him to remember and release,

Is because I'm afraid to know he was ever so vulnerable;
Almost locked-up. Almost thrown away. Almost buried, forever.

## *A Poem Where I try to Make Sense out of Diaspora and Assimilation*

I've written plenty of poems about my parents' sacrifice for our family.
But can there ever truly be enough? I always end up feeling ungrateful

for being American. Guilty for simply being happy or publishing a book,
when my folks didn't have such opportunities. Then again,

I know this is why they came to this country. For me to thrive.
For me to write this book. For me to read in front of a crowd of strangers.

My folks aren't perfect, no one is. In fact, the first-gen struggle
often pits folks against each other. We've all heard the parable

of the crabs in a barrel, right? Where a single crab tries to rise
out of a bucket only to be pulled down by fellow crabs.

We must remember not to be loaded weapons aimed at each other.
It is easy to blame your brother when you're both starving.

My goal is to eventually have my parents see their sacrifice as worth it.
Not just for the education, wealth, and prosperity, but so they can see

it wasn't at the expense of family unity.

## Sports Cards

When I was a kid, maybe eight or ten years old,
my brothers, friends, and I would steal sports cards
from the local Kmart. I knew it was wrong and I felt guilty,

but at the same time, I didn't have the money for it.
Don't get me wrong, every now and then,
my parents would give me money and I'd buy cards,

but it was never enough to fill my desire for sports cards.
We would put the packs of cards in our pockets.
Then we'd walk out of the store, undetected.

I feel so bad telling this story now, almost thirty years later;
I should've known better. All I wanted was a Kobe Bryant
rookie card. Or a Ken Griffey Jr. rookie card.

Is that so much to ask? Can't a first-generation, poor kid
steal his dreams, if he can't afford them?

## The Seventh Grade

Was the first time I kissed a girl. Her name was Jasmine.
She was the wildest kid in school. No father.

She would ditch, smoke cigarettes, and hang out
With high school kids. But she was pretty,

So, I let her kiss me. We weren't even going out,
But I didn't mind her kissing me after 7th period.

She would stick her whole tongue down my throat.
I didn't really even know what I was doing,

But I liked it. I can't lie. Some of the other kids
Asked if she was my girlfriend, but I just said

We were friends. Jasmine ended up hooked on meth
For a while. I never saw her after junior high.

Hope she is happy somewhere. Somewhere safe.

*Self-Portrait of Southeast L.A.*

Riding the bus up Imperial Hwy,
    to the Weaver Library, I peer out
of the graffiti-laced windows and see a piñata
      dangling from the tall branches of a willow tree

    at Independence Park. I know I am southeast of the
artificial river—
it is written in invisible ink on the dusty shop windows
    where Virgencitas and Mexican and American flags
hang like ornaments on Christmas trees. I know I am southeast—

it can be smelled inside Gonzalez Market where the aroma
    del bolillo fresco meshes with the chisme and chatter
of the Spanglish day. I know I am southeast of the American
river—
    it is written on my juxtaposed, Chicano stare,

    as I shift perspective from outside the window to inside:
where immigrants commute to work, some without driver's
licenses:
    A law that must change with the evolving city.
A city built by immigrants for all to thrive.

## *The Santa Fe Springs Swap Meet*

A man in a Durand Jones & The Indications shirt went to the Santa Fe Springs Swap Meet in Southeast Los Angeles on a Friday night with his primos. The first stop was the long line for Micheladas. They listened to a Santana cover band on the main stage. They nodded their heads to the smooth music. After they got their drinks, they walked around the various vendors and bought a wallet and hats of their favorite teams: Lakers. Dodgers. Rams. Palm trees swayed in the warm moonlight. The 5-freeway roared in the background. The man in a Durand Jones & The Indications shirt took a photo of a mural of Canelo Alvarez vs Gennady Golovkin, "Triple G." At the end of the night, they went to In-N-Out on the other side of the freeway. They had combo #2's animal style. Summer was nearly over, so they were glad to have visited the swap meet before it became too cold at night. Honestly, the swap meet was always a go-to chill spot for all the locals.

## Guanajuato, México

When I was in my mid-twenties, fresh out of undergrad, not knowing what I wanted to do with my life, I visited Guanajuato, México, my parents' home state, with my older brother and mom. I hadn't been back since childhood. At first, I felt odd, like I stood out, introvert that I was. Then, I visited the mercado, full of locals and colorful piñatas. It was comforting just walking around with the locals, mi gente. We bought fruta in a cup with chili and lime. I bought a pirated jersey of my favorite Mexican League soccer team, León. Mis primos took me to different family parties, discotecas, and even to a local bookstore upon my request. The whole time I was in México, I felt like I was returning home, in a way. At moments, I felt like I didn't stand out anymore, like in America, at least not physically. I was just another Brown man, Brown hands, Brown face, in my ancient land, but with an American accent. Some Mexicans did seem fascinated by my SoCal swagger and surfer clothes, though. When we ultimately said goodbye to our familia before heading to the airport, I was in tears, we all were. I haven't seen my Guanajuato familia since then, in more than ten years. I'd like to return soon, but they say it's dangerous right now. One day, I'll return, though, I know it, like the dahlias in spring.

III

*My Kafka Prose Poem*

I woke up and logged onto Twitter to discover someone
impersonating me. They said I like to read novels in the bathtub,
but I don't have the attention span for that, and, besides, I only
take showers. They posted things with swagger and confidence,
instead of second-guessing and qualifying every thought like
I do. They created another personality for me, one who doesn't
feel guilty about going to Starbucks, Amazon, or other corporate
chains; a care-free everyman, one could say.

When I reported this to Twitter Support, they said I was
the actual fraud. That my name doesn't match with my ID card.
I told them that's because it's my pen name and my mother's
maiden name as well. They told me to take a hike and get a real
job because writing is a form of criminality. I now wander the
damp streets looking for my past self. The one with 25K followers
and a sense of purpose. Follow me, dear friends, beneath the
scattered moonlight. I'm craving Starbucks, again, but the real me
actually feels guilty about it.

## I Wasn't Lionel Messi

I turned the calendar in my downtown apartment, and it was New Year's Day. I had somehow forgotten my entire past, childhood included. I didn't even recall my name. Was it David? I looked like a David with my pious haircut. Was it David de la Cruz? No, it wasn't. Ronaldo? Leonardo? Leo? Was I Lionel Messi? No, I wasn't. I was, though, in denial. Perhaps of some accentuated failures. My inability to study Law. My languid approach to language. My longing for Prima Ballerinas and tenured professors in the Humanities or Poetry, Western Philosophy aka the depressive arts. No, I would never be Lionel Messi. I had never scored two goals against France. Try as I did.

## Bilingual Jingle

I speak two languages, one of them, fluently. The other, I'm improving, daily, if I remember to study. I practice by singing along to epic Rancheras about lost romance and decaying rosas. Also, sometimes I'll read modernist Spanish poetry about fractured skies and Pablo Picasso's crooked eyes. I love the Spanish language when a beautiful woman tells me, querido te quiero mucho muchisimo queridisimo, I could hear that all day. If I were a Spanish Baroque painter, like Diego Velázquez, I'd paint better than I sing in Spanish which would be pretty damn good because I'm a celebrated singer. Sunday night karaoke nights at the local mariscos cantina are always lit.

## *The Grandfather Clock*

A man got stuck inside a grandfather clock at the public library. He had just been sitting there minding his own business, on a rocking chair, reading Baudelaire, when all the sudden he was stuck. Had he shrunk? Did the clock grow bigger? He felt essentially the same, except for a tension in his neck and a growing claustrophobia. He began to count the numbers on the clock to remain sane: 1, 2, 3, 4, 5, 6, who was he kidding? He was doomed. Destined to spend the rest of his life inside of an old clock.

Then the clock struck midnight. Ring-Ring-Ring! The man jolted awake. The clock was nowhere to be found. He wasn't even at the library anymore. In fact, he was sitting next to a blank canvas with an easel and brush. He began to paint an old grandfather clock . . .

*The Gym*

A man went to the gym on his day off from work. He works as
a librarian in the city. He was organizing a set of books about
exercise when he decided he needed to start going to the gym.
First, he ran on the treadmill for forty-five minutes. He felt alive.
Then, he worked out on the bench press. He felt good. Finally, the
man swam in the pool and then relaxed in the jacuzzi. When
he got home, he read a book about Salvador Dali's paintings of
giraffes, elephants, and dreams. He fell asleep like a sloth in a tree.

## The Woman with Flowers in Her Hair

There was a woman who was born with flowers in her hair. When she was a baby, they were tiny pink roses. As she grew, more diverse flowers sprouted in her hair. Dahlias, dandelions, lilacs. The woman with flowers in her hair could not go anywhere without unwanted attention, glares. The townspeople called her "Flower Woman." She cried at night, tears of loneliness.

One day, the woman noticed a pink rose falling from her hair. The next day an orchid fell. By the end of the year the woman no longer had any flowers in her hair. She was overjoyed! She danced for days. She found a boyfriend. He turned into a husband. She started a family. She was ecstatic!

But it didn't last. She thought she would completely adore freedom. The sense of fitting in with the background. However, she couldn't deny it, she missed the flowers in her hair. She missed the colorful way she looked in the mirror. She missed the dahlias and the lilacs, the dandelions. Most of all, she missed the smell of flowers when it rained.

*Fresh Flowers*

I was walking in a forest when I found a book of prose poems
by Charles Baudelaire floating in a calm creek. I knelt into the
shallow water and grabbed the book. It was signed by Baudelaire
himself, or, just as likely, a forged copy. Nevertheless, I placed the
book onto a patch of soft grass beneath the summer sun. It dried
with the light breeze like a surfer resting in the sand after an early
morning session.

After an hour, I picked up the book and began to read. I
read for about three hours. Then, the moon came up like a wish.
I fell asleep in the field, by the creek, with the book on my chest.
The next morning when the sun woke me, the book was gone. I
was confused for a moment, until I saw the book floating back
in the creek. I dug it out, once more, and dried it off, again. I
continued reading, by the creek. The French words, poems, and
soft pages were like fresh flowers to me. Time became irrelevant.

## Blue Lobster Soliloquy

1 in 5,000 North Atlantic lobsters are born bright blue. Sometimes, I wish I was born bright blue. But then, no, I can't decide. To be famous, infamous or just blend in with the crowd? Which is better? Aren't we all essentially the same, anyway? Who decides all of these random circumstances we are born into? No one? God? Mary? The lambs? No one, right? Random occurrence, right? That's where we're at in history, I'm assuming. Anyway, a bright blue lobster, how romantic. Poetic. Normal. Iconoclastic. Mundane. Obscure. Either way, I'm hungry, where's that peculiar lobster?

## Domesticated Beasts

I was in a cheerful mood, so I went to the zoo at the edge of the city. I laughed at a comic book with the idyllic zebras. I slow-danced to Chopin with the lavish gorillas. I sang a Spanish ballad to the stylish flamingos. At the end of the visit, I took a much-needed nap by the tortoise enclosure. When I woke up, there was a baby tortoise crawling along my back. I gently placed the young tortoise back into the enclosure. As I left the zoo and walked to the bus stop, I remembered tomorrow would be my 38th birthday. A perfect place to spend it, I thought, the zoo, with similarly domesticated beasts.

## The Man in a Reindeer Mask

I was having a cup of plain coffee by myself at a café downtown when a man in a reindeer mask entered and approached my table. He said he was raising money for the dying rain forests throughout the world. I told him all the money I had I spent on coffee and that I was sorry I couldn't help. He proceeded to read me a Haiku he'd written. It was about the rainforest and the vanishing trees. I told him I appreciated the sentiment of his Haiku. When he saw I genuinely had no money, we shook hands, and he left. The man in a reindeer mask exited the coffee shop and boarded a busy bus. I thought about the brevity and beauty of his Haiku all day, though. And the next day and week as well. A fading rainforest. A lone deer. The utter void.

## *The Summer I was Good Friends with Salvador Dalí and Diego Maradona*

I was having coffee with Salvador Dalí and Diego Maradona at
a hippie coffee shop in Venice Beach one summer. Dalí insisted
on having black tea. He said he "already is drugs" or something
subversive. They both said I sounded American. "Well, I was born
in America, I tell them. But I'm Latino. Mexican American," I say.
I ask Dalí who his favorite soccer team is. "La Barcelona," he says,
as he examines the marigolds on the coffee table. I ask Maradona
who is his favorite painter? "La Frida Kahlo," he says.

After we finish our coffees, we walk along the Venice coast.
Suddenly, Maradona dives into the ocean. He swims alongside
a dolphin and a local surfer. Dalí and I laugh out loud. Later, we
lay on the sand and watch the sunset. At the end of the night, the
moon comes up like a seagull on a streetlamp. We go to a local
bar called The Clam and talk politics and literature with local
lady surfers. I tell them my name is Roberto Durán, former world
champion. We have a good laugh as we drink our Mexican beers
and dance the night away to cumbias.

## The Dragon and the Carnival

I was riding the Ferris wheel at the local carnival. It was the
end of summer and the new semester was on the horizon. I
had learned a lot since I first started teaching medieval sword
fighting to college students in the suburbs of Los Angeles. It was
an inspiring experience. A rebirth one could say. After about the
fourth spin around on the Ferris wheel, I began to doze off. It felt
like a deep sleep, but it was just a few minutes.

Anyway, when I woke up, a large forest-green dragon
approached the small carnival. It was a medieval dragon from
another century. I quickly exited the Ferris wheel. I pulled out
my sword and mounted my nearby horse. I charged the dragon. I
had no other option. Besides, I was a skilled swordsman. All my
students knew it. The dragon was a worthy opponent, though. I
dodged its flames from its nostrils like a swan darting around a
summer lake. Finally, I dug my sword into the dragon's obtrusive
skull, and I stood on its beating chest. The dragon puffed a final
breath. Eventually, the midnight moon rose above the suburbs of
Southeast Los Angeles.

## *The Fireman*

I fell from a ten-foot ladder as I was trying to rescue my kitten from a willow tree. I fell into a pile of old wrinkled love poems I had written in youth to a young woman I had a crush on back in undergrad. I refused to ask her out back then, due to extreme shyness, so instead I wrote her dramatic imitations of Petrarchan love sonnets, which, of course, I never sent her.

As I picked myself up off the ground, I noticed the kitten had transformed into Margot Cisneros, the young woman I had a crush on back in undergrad. I asked her out, finally. Now was my chance. Now, that I was a man. She said she was happily married, a nurse, and not a fan of poetry. I told her, *but I'm not a poet, I'm a fireman, don't you see me rescuing you with my axe from this giant willow tree?* And we lived happily ever after. The four of us, Margot, the kitten, the willow tree, and me.

## A Wednesday in Autumn Where I Turn into Pinocchio at the Local Library

I was teaching an online class at the library on the decay of western civilization when the librarian rushed in and told me my time was up. I pleaded for another five minutes in vain. I was just getting to the good stuff. The petite librarian proceeded to get me in a headlock and escorted me off the premises. She told me I was a bad seed. When I asked for my wallet she denounced me as a rebel without a cause. I tried to forget about it as I walked home in the rain, wallet less. It was a record rainfall, lately. But we were in a drought, so I was actually grateful. I noticed a slick puddle adjacent to the graffitied sewer and saw my worn reflection. I was somehow growing donkey ears and a tail. Was I turning into a donkey like Pinocchio when he lied? Who was Gepetto? The librarian? I hadn't told a lie. What lie had I uttered? I had denounced western civilization, but I was merely being sardonic. Nevertheless, I take it back, I don't want to be a donkey anymore. The rain suddenly stopped. I opened the door to my rickety apartment. It was my birthday on the weekend. Everything would be all right, right? Everything, except the trauma inflicted by the petite librarian. No worries, though, I'd paint it all away, like everything else. It had worked before, it'd work again. No sweat, really.

## The Museum of Mirrors

A man in a Pink Floyd shirt walked in the rain. It was Wednesday afternoon. Nothing mattered. He jumped onto a bus bench. He recited a few of Shakespeare's sonnets from memory, out loud, in the rain. Some folks laughed. Others listened intently beneath their umbrellas. When the man in a Pink Floyd shirt finished, he caught a bus to a museum, downtown. It was a museum of mirrors. Everyone was important at the museum of mirrors. Everyone was a Picasso or Van Gogh. He took plenty of photographs or technically mirror selfies at the museum of mirrors. At the end of the night, the man in a Pink Floyd shirt caught a cab home, as the driver played Rachmaninoff beneath the moonlight.

≈ IV ≈

*Among the Flowers: Ballet in the City*

A man in a Frida Kahlo shirt painted onto the side of a giant skyscraper in Downtown Los Angeles. He painted the terse wall with an assortment of roses, lilacs, and dahlias. The man in a Frida Kahlo shirt was being commissioned by The Los Angeles Ballet Company to paint a mural advertisement for an upcoming winter show. After he painted the dazzling flowers, he painted in two skillful Black and Brown dancers: one in the air, the other holding them. The dancers swayed among the flowers on the historic skyscraper in the middle of the city. When the man in a Frida Kahlo shirt finished painting the mural, he titled it: *Among the Flowers: Ballet in the City.*

## The City Is Dead Without Your Pirouette of a Smile

A man in an MF DOOM shirt skated in the city. He ollied over a trash can. He picked up a leaf and put it in his pocket. The man in an MF DOOM shirt skated by the Opera House. There was a ballet going on. He went inside and enjoyed the show. He used to date a Russian-American Ballerina. They had known each other since childhood. One day she left him for a Spanish Ballerino. He never felt so alone. As he watched the ballet, he started to write a poem. It was called, "The City Is Dead Without Your Pirouette of a Smile."

## The Lilac Wind

A man in an MF DOOM shirt rode the bus to an art gallery. He was going to see his favorite graffiti artist: The Lilac Wind. The Lilac Wind was an obscure painter who never showed his face in public, like DOOM, like Banksy. As he rode the bus, he wondered who it could be?

The doors opened at 8 p.m., sharp. The man in an MF DOOM shirt ran to the front of the line. As he walked around the gallery, he noticed nothing but painted canvases full of words dripping with paint: Revolver. Evolve. Solution. Ignite. Recycle. Breath. Repeat. Align. Forgive. Teach.—The Lilac Wind. The man in an MF DOOM shirt sat in awe. He didn't care who the man actually was anymore. It could've been any of a number of these artsy types, he thought. What matters is the words dripping with bright paint on the canvases. He rode the bus home as the moon rose over the city and he thought of the final two words on the final canvases: Believe. Exist.

## EL CHACAL

A man in an MF DOOM shirt known as "El Chacal" walked
downtown in the city. "El Chacal" was looking for his favorite
street taco vendor. The vendor sold tacos de asada, el pastor, and
Coca Colas. The man in an MF DOOM shirt, "El Chacal," was
masked: a virus had spread that winter. *It will all be over soon,*
he thought. Downtown, the city was a Ghost Town. He began
to realize the taco vendor wouldn't be there, either. "El Chacal"
pivoted and rode the empty subway car back to his apartment on
the southeast side of the city. As he exited the train, he resisted an
innate urge to tag on the train's window in all caps: "EL CHACAL."

*The Ice Cream Sandwich at the End of the World*

A man in an MF DOOM shirt woke up in the middle of the
night and wrote a poem. The poem was about a dragon who
had polluted the city with his flames. The dragon was trying to
destroy the city: a modern metropolis. The dragon rode around
in an old Chevy engulfing the city in flames. As he wrote the
poem, the man in an MF DOOM shirt described the dragon, "A
purple dragon with teeth like a snake and wings like a bat." He
described how the dragon drove around the city, "The dragon
cruised in tough and quiet neighborhoods alike and set fire to
the world." Just as he was about to write the ending, or the death
of the dragon, the man in an MF DOOM shirt fell back asleep.
This time he dreamed about eating an ice cream sandwich at the
aforementioned end of the world.

## The Barn Swallow

I finished drawing a barn swallow onto a canvas and began
mixing paint to color it in. I mixed blue and grey for the head
and wings, and brown and orange for the chest. When I finished
painting in the bird, it began to suddenly flap its wings. I jumped
back. I wasn't sure if it was real or a strange dream. I hid behind
my desk and waited. The barn swallow then let out a piercing
"cheep, cheep!" I grabbed a tennis racket in case it came after me.
After a couple minutes of observing the bird from behind my desk,
I realized it wasn't real. It was some sort of audible hologram. I
lit a cigarette. In order to set it free, I walked up to the canvas,
dipped my brush in azure blue, and painted in a sky.

## *The Seagull*

The seagull flew over the ocean and back to its home on the beach. The seagull stood on the edge of the pier and watched the sea. The seagull almost crashed into a palm tree in the middle of the night. The seagull walked along the shore as waves crashed at its feet. The seagull walked past napping sea lions on the slippery pier. The seagull was sketched onto a helmet of a high school football team. The seagull once flew to Antarctica on a dare from a pirate. At sunset, the seagull slept in the sand in the middle of the beach.

## The Palm Tree

The palm tree stood on the beach and laughed at the sea. The palm tree: juxtaposed with a seagull, sun, and the clouds. The palm tree was tattooed onto the arm of a motorcycle vandal. The palm tree recalled the pink sunset of another century. The palm tree is light. The palm tree must not be forsaken in the heat of the night. The palm tree has roots. The palm tree is mine. The palm tree grew wings. The palm tree can fly.

## *José Emilio Pacheco's Ghost and the Flying Jaguar*

I was at a hidden local beach in Southern California away from the tourist traps of Santa Monica and Huntington Beach. The sun was shining but it wasn't overwhelming; it was still early in the morning. That's when I saw a flying jaguar in the late spring sky. It approached the sand and landed a few feet away from me. I was in shock. I forgot to mention that riding the flying jaguar was none other than José Emilio Pacheco's ghost. Had I accidentally taken hallucinogenic drugs? No, I mean I had Starbucks for breakfast but everything was checking out as normal. Pacheco descended from the winged jaguar and asked my name. "My name is Jose Hernandez Diaz," I mumbled. "Are you from around here?" he continued. "Yes, I am. I'm from Southeast Los Angeles. I used to be from Orange County . . . The real question is what are you doing on a flying jaguar? You died years ago," I said. "I've come to remind you to read more Spanish language poetry," he said. "You'll grow to love it just as much as your first language." "Technically, Spanish is my first language," I said, "I learned it alongside English from my parents as a young boy but quickly switched to English because it was easier. You make a good point about me speaking more Spanish, Señor Pacheco," I said. "I promise to work on it." But just as I said this, Pacheco and the flying jaguar disappeared. I grabbed my longboard and headed to my car. I left the beach and went to the library to check out Pacheco's books, bilingual editions.

*Hey,*

With the intention of going to an independent bookstore
with you, both of us fed up with the machinery of capitalism,

consumption, the greed. Hey, with the intention of filling the void
with your smile, your laugh, your kiss beneath the autumn moon.

Hey, with the intention of moving to Montana with you,
writing and painting, inspired by the muse of the mundane,

living a minimalist lifestyle, until they grant us both MacArthur Grants,
and we can afford to fly away to the Moon.

# BIOGRAPHIC NOTE

Jose Hernandez Diaz is a 2017 NEA Poetry Fellow. He is the author of *The Fire Eater* (Texas Review Press, 2020), *Bad Mexican, Bad American* (Acre Books, 2024), and *The Parachutist* (Sundress Publications, 2025). He has been published in the *Yale Review*, the *London Magazine*, and in the *Southern Review*. He teaches generative workshops for Hugo House, Lighthouse Writers Workshops, The Writer's Center, and elsewhere. Additionally, he serves as a Poetry Mentor in The Adroit Journal Summer Mentorship Program. He is from Norwalk, California.